FAANGMULA

REAL-LIFE SHORT STORIES FROM COMPUTER SCIENCE INDUSTRY & RESEARCH COMMUNITY

Story Book for Programmers

First Edition

Aditya Chatterjee ✤ Ue Kiao ✤ Geoffrey Ziskovin

 **OPENGENUS**

BE A NATIONAL PROGRAMMER

HAVE A REAL-LIFE HISTORIC STORY TO ADD?

Email us at team@opengenus.org and get yourself added as a contributor.

INTRODUCTION

Enjoy your time with this book.

This book "**FAANGMULA**" is the best book a developer reads in her or his leisure time for entertainment. This book is a collection of real-life short stories from the history of Computer Science Industry and Research Community.

Get started with this book and enjoy while you grow your career.

Book: **FAANGMULA: Real-life short stories from Computer Science Industry and Research Community**

Authors (3): Aditya Chatterjee, Ue Kiao, Geoffrey Ziskovin

About the authors:

Aditya Chatterjee is an Independent Researcher, Technical Author and the Founding Member of OPENGENUS, a scientific community focused on Computing Technology.

Ue Kiao is a Japanese Software Developer and has played key role in designing systems like TaoBao, AliPay and many more. She has completed her B. Sc in Mathematics and Computing Science at National Taiwan University and PhD at Tokyo Institute of Technology.

Geoffrey Ziskovin is an American Software Engineer with an experience of over 30 years. He has interviewed over 700 candidates worldwide for various Fortune 500 companies.

Published: 17 May 2024 (Edition 1)

ISBN: 9798333678966

Publisher: © OpenGenus

Contact: team@opengenus.org

Available on Amazon as E-book and Paperback.

Images included in this book are under CC BY-SA 3.0 license.

CC BY-SA 3.0: creativecommons.org/licenses/by-sa/3.0

© All rights reserved. No textual part of this book should be reproduced or distributed without written permission from the authors and OpenGenus.

SHORT STORIES

Story of Multiplication 7
Turing's lost silver in WWII 16
Flight Crash in 40 seconds due to 16-bit overflow 18
Patriot Missile Failure (1991 Gulf War) 21
NASA's Mars Climate Orbiter missing since 1999............. 25
PageRank Patent 29
Most Profitable Software Patents 32
Origin of Git 36
Sad Story of Gerrit 37
Google vs Oracle: 10 years long battle 39
Pentium Floating Point Division bug................................. 41
Apple's breakup with Intel after 15 years 44

Story of Multiplication

The story of doing multiplication is interesting.

Everyone knows how to multiply 2 integers and this was the only known method for centuries. In terms of time complexity, if the numbers have N bits, then the time complexity of multiplication will be $O(N^2)$.

This was assumed to be a universal truth.

Moscow Mathematical Society

The story goes back to 1956 in a meeting at **Moscow Mathematical Society**.

In 1956, Andrey Nikolaevich Kolmogorov was the president of the society and a prominent Soviet mathematician who was well known for his discoveries. He had **created the idea of Time Complexity** and formulated a conjecture that the lower estimate for the number of operations for Multiplication of N bit numbers is of the order of N^2.

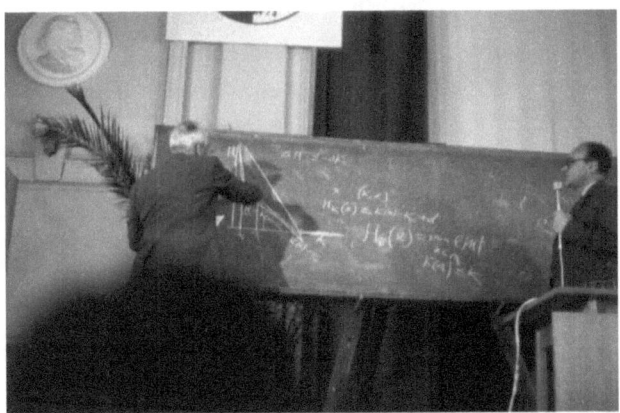

Kolmogorov (left) delivering a talk in 1970s.

The conjecture was named **Kolmogorov's Conjecture**.

This was going to be proved wrong in just 4 years with a week's work which led to several unexpected events.

In the 1956, discussions happened on this and mathematicians noted that in decimal number system, the conjecture is true. For other systems like the Czech method of representing numbers, it may not be valid. The Czech method was suggested by Svoboda and Valach.

Entry of Karatsuba as an attendee

In **1960**, a seminar was held in Faculty of Mechanics and Mathematics at **Moscow University under the guidance of Kolmogorov**. Kolmogorov N^2 conjecture and complexity of linear systems were presented.

Karatsuba was a student at that time.

Anatoly Alexeyevich Karatsuba

Over the weekend, Karatsuba developed an algorithm for Multiplication with a Time Complexity of less than $O(N^2)$. More specifically, the Time Complexity of Karatsuba Algorithm is $O(N^{\log 3}) = O(N^{1.5849...})$. It was based on divide and conquer approach.

In the next seminar which was after a week, Karatsuba informed Kolmogorov of his new algorithm and how his conjecture is wrong.

How Kolmogorov reacted?

Kolmogorov was disappointed as his conjecture "Kolmogorov N^2 conjecture" was the main focus of his seminars and was an active area of research in Time Complexity.

Multiplication was considered to be a difficult problem and his conjecture was assumed to be very difficult to prove or disprove if not considered to be true.

This was a setback for Kolmogorov as he was a leading figure in this field.

In the next seminar following the current seminar where Karatsuba and Kolmogorov discussed, Kolmogorov talked about Karatsuba's discovery. **This was the last time Kolmogorov and Karatsuba met or talked**.

Kolmogorov abruptly ended the seminar mid-way and never talked about his conjecture and Karatsuba's algorithm ever again.

Suddenly 2 years later in **1962**, Kolmogorov submitted a paper in the name of Karatsuba and Ofman. Ofman was a student of Kolmogorov.

This raised a controversy that Kolmogorov published Karatsuba's work including other researchers who were not involved. This is a toxic practice in the research community but in this case, it was mentioned in the paper that it was Karatsuba's work solely.

Karatsuba was unaware of the publication of this paper and **got to know about it after 2 years in 1964**.

This is how the events unfolded:

- In 1956, Kolmogorov formed Kolmogorov N^2 conjecture which was a major point in his seminars and in the field of Time Complexity.
- In 1960, Kolmogorov planned to conduct seminars in Moscow University.
- In his first seminar, he explained his conjecture along with other problems.
- In the second seminar, Karatsuba informed Kolmogorov that his conjecture was wrong.
- In third seminar, Kolmogorov talked about Karatsuba's findings.
- Kolmogorov ended the seminar without any notice and never contacted Karatsuba ever after this day.
- In 1962 (after 2 years), Kolmogorov published Karatsuba's work in name of Karatsuba and Ofman (his student) without informing Karatsuba.

This was a major breakthrough.

Karatsuba algorithm was the first algorithm to show that Integer Multiplication can be done faster than $O(N^2)$ at a time when scientists where stuck in this field for centuries.

The next progress was made quickly in **1963** by coming up with Toom Cook multiplication. It had a time complexity of $O(N^{1.46})$.

This field was in active research and the news of recent progress spread like wild fire. Just last 3 years made a huge impact in the field which shook everyone for decades.

In 1971, Schonhage Strassen algorithm was designed which remained the **fastest Integer Multiplication algorithm for over 36 years**.

Schonhage Strassen algorithm had a time complexity of O(N logN loglogN) time.

The record was broken in 2007 by Furer's algorithm. From then, progress has been over the constant factor only.

Furer's algorithm was a **major breakthrough as no fundamental progress was made from 1971 to 2007**. It showed that further progress is possible. It improved the time complexity to O(N logN 2O(log*N)).

It improved the loglogN part of Schonhage Strassen algorithm which is true **for large numbers such as 2264**.

Despite this, it remains of theoretical interest only because of several significant challenges to make its use in practical applications. This opened up a whole new interest in the domain and in the following years several optimizations where proposed but none made it suitable for practical use. Hence, **Schonhage Strassen algorithm continued to be used in all practical uses.**

Several improvements on Furer's Algorithms have been done since 2007.

DKSS Algorithm was a notable approach as it achieved the same time complexity as Furer's algorithm. It relied on modular arithmetic and is simpler. It came out in 2008 and has a time complexity of O(N logN 2O(log*N)). This is faster than Schonhage Strassen algorithm for **numbers greater than 10104796**.

In 2015, Harvey, Hoeven, Lecerf came up with an algorithm with a better bounded constant as compared to Furer's Algorithm. It relied on Messene primes and had a time complexity of O(N logN 23 log*N) where the constant is 3 while in Furer's algorithm, it is not bounded and can be larger like 8.

Soon, Covanov and Thomé in the same year 2015, came up with another algorithm based on Fermat Primes and improved the constant factor to 2. The time complexity improved to O(N * logN * 22 log*N).

Despite these improvements, the algorithms were not suitable for practical use and minimal improvements were being made. To a positive note, we have several algorithms with different basic ideas.

The next ground breaking discovery was made in **March 2019** by Harvey and van der Hoeven. They have proposed an algorithm with time complexity of **O(N logN)**. This is significant as in 1971, Volker Strassen said that the possible best complexity for Integer Multiplication should be O(N logN) and we have reached the possible end.

Harvey explaining approaches to Multiplication.

Though several different approaches will come in years to follow, we have come a long way and optimized this fundamental operation to its limit.

Following summarizes the algorithms that defined this era:

ALGORITHM	COMPLEXITY	YEAR	NOTES
School Multiplication	$O(N^2)$	100 BC	-
Russian Peasant Method	$O(N^2 * \log N)$	1000 AD	-
Karatsuba algorithm	$O(N^{1.58})$	1960	-

ALGORITHM	COMPLEXITY	YEAR	NOTES
Toom Cook multiplication	$O(N^{1.46})$	1963	-
Schonhage Strassen algorithm	$O(N * \log N * \log\log N)$	1971	FFT
Furer's algorithm	$O(N * \log N * 2^{O(\log^* N)})$	2007	-
DKSS Algorithm	$O(N * \log N * 2^{O(\log^* N)})$	2008	Modular arithmetic
Harvey, Hoeven, Lecerf	$O(N * \log N * 2^{3 \log^* N})$	2015	Mersenne primes
Covanov and Thomé	$O(N * \log N * 2^{2 \log^* N})$	2015	Fermat primes
Harvey and van der Hoeven	$O(N * \log N)$	March 2019	Possible end

Turing's lost silver in WWII

Everyone is concerned about their belongings.

Alan Turing was a British mathematician, logician, and cryptanalyst and is often, considered as the "**Father of Modern Computing**".

During World War II, Alan Turing was deeply concerned about the possibility of a Nazi invasion of Britain. As a precaution, he decided to bury a collection of silver bars in the woods near his wartime workplace at Bletchley Park.

The location

Alan Turing was near Bletchley Park because he was one of the key members of the **Government Code and Cypher School (GC&CS)** during World War II.

A building in Bletchley Park

Bletchley Park, located in Buckinghamshire, England, was chosen as the central site for British codebreakers, due to its secluded yet accessible location. Turing, already recognized for his mathematical prowess and expertise in cryptography, was recruited to join the team of cryptanalysts tasked with breaking enemy codes.

Hiding the treasure

Turing meticulously planned the burial, creating an intricate map and a detailed code to ensure he could locate the silver bars later.

Lost treasure

When the threat of invasion subsided, Turing attempted to retrieve his buried treasure but found himself unable to remember the exact location or decode his own encryption.

The code Turing used was characteristically complex, involving a cipher that he believed only he could decode. Despite his brilliance, Turing's attention to the code and map was so meticulous that it eventually became too complex even for him to decipher.

The silver bars remained lost.

Bletchley Park has been preserved as a heritage site and museum hence, you cannot go digging in search for it.

Flight Crash in 40 seconds due to 16-bit overflow

A simple overflow led to a loss of $370M

17 seconds before launch.

It may be hard to imagine that an expensive system will fail for an overflow error in 1996 when the World had over 40 years of Programming experience but it did happen.

It was **Ariane 501 rocket** which crashed on 4 June 1996 in Kourou, French Guiana (in South America) just 40 seconds after launch.

It failed due to a software error in the inertial reference system's guidance and control software (SRI). The error occurred when the software **attempted to convert a 64-bit floating-point number to a 16-bit signed integer**, causing an overflow error that shut down the rocket's guidance system (SRI).

The greater horizontal acceleration was the 64-bit number. The on-board computers **interpreted the rocket was 90 degrees off course**.

Example: the 64-bit number **6028463252429544** results in **-9496** in 16-bits (2's complement).

64-bit number: 0000000000010101011010101101101011110101011001 11101101011101000

16-bit: **1**101101011101000

As most significant bit is 1, 2's complement is used which results in the value **-9496**.

The SRI software received an unexpected value for the launcher's horizontal velocity, which caused an unhandled exception.

The rocket took a 90 degree turn and exploded.

This caused the rocket to veer off course 37 seconds after launch, at an altitude of 3,700 meters, and experience aerodynamic stress that tore its boosters from the main stage. The rocket then self-destructed in a fireball of liquid hydrogen, costing approximately **$370 million**.

Patriot Missile Failure (1991 Gulf War)

On 25 February 1991, Iraq successfully launched a Scud missile that hit a U.S. Army barracks near Dhahran, Saudi Arabia. It resulted in 28 deaths and over 70 serious injuries. It was the last Scud fired in the Gulf War.

The last Dhahran Scud succeeded due to a software error in the Patriot missile defense system which was responsible for hitting the missiles mid-air. The problem was in the calculations were an error in calculating the position of the scud accumulated over time resulting in a large error.

The Patriot missile defense system used a **24-bit CPU** based on a 1970 architecture.

The software was written in Assembly. Real numbers were stored in 2 24-bit registers where one register was for the integer part and second register was for the fractional part. The system time was updated by the system's internal clock every tenth of a second. This results in an error as 1/10 cannot be represented exactly in a binary system.

The algorithm was as follows:

- Check if object might be a Scud missile in the 3-D radar sweep data.

- For each possible Scud, calculate expected next location at the known speed of a Scud (+/- an acceptable window).
- Check the radar sweep data again at the calculated future time to see if the object is in the location a Scud would be.
- If it is a Scud, fix target and fire missiles.

A Patriot missile defense system from Israel in 2017

The Government report on the error noted an accumulating error of 0.003433 seconds per 1 hour of uptime. Let us understand this with a simple calculation:

The binary expansion of 1/10 is
0.0001100110011001100110011001100....

A 24-bit register will store it as
0.00011001100110011001100 (first 24 bits) introducing an error of 0.00000000000000000000000**11001100**... (remaining part in the actual representation) in binary, or about 0.000000**95** in decimal. Multiplying by the number of tenths of a second in 100 hours gives 0.000000095×100×60×60×10 = 0.3420

A Scud travelling at a speed of 1,676 meters per second will travel **569.84 meters**. This means the missile was 0.5 Km ahead or behind the target. This was far enough that the incoming Scud was outside the "range gate" that the Patriot tracked.

Hence, the missile escaped and caused massive damage.

The interesting thing is that Iraq had launched around 70 such missiles before this and all were stopped successfully and **this was the last missile Iraq had**.

Developers used to send software patches to update the system in every few days and the **updating process took up to 2 hours**. Rebooting took up to 90 seconds so it was costly as well but it used to set the accumulated time to 0.

Moreover, 4 days before, the developers informed that there is a accumulation error and it can cause errors. To avoid it, the system should be rebooted whenever possible.

As the war was in peak, the system was kept running for over 100 hours which accumulated in the error.

The next day the developers had send the patch to fix this accumulation error. Little did they know, the damage was already done.

NASA's Mars Climate Orbiter missing since 1999

Kids are taught in school that we cannot compare temperatures in Celsius and Fahrenheit but NASA engineers missed this in 1999.

Mars Climate Orbiter waiting to undergo a spin test in 1998

The Mars Climate Orbiter was part of NASA's Mars Surveyor program, designed to study the Martian climate, atmosphere, and surface from orbit.

Mars Climate Orbiter undergoing acoustic testing

The orbiter was equipped with scientific instruments and was critical for gathering data on Mars' atmosphere and weather patterns.

It was launched on **December 11, 1998**, with a planned arrival at Mars in **September 1999**.

As the orbiter approached Mars, a series of trajectory correction maneuvers were planned to adjust its course for orbital insertion around the planet.

Just when NASA was about to announce the successful mission, the **orbiter went missing**. There are 2 possible theories of where it went:

- was destroyed in the Martian atmosphere

- or, escaped the planet's vicinity and entered an orbit around the Sun.

After investigation, NASA found the issue.

During the mission planning phase, engineers at **Lockheed Martin**, the spacecraft's manufacturer, used imperial units (pounds-force-seconds) for thrust measurements in navigation software.

Lockheed Martin is a leading Aerospace and defense company.

On the other hand, NASA's Jet Propulsion Laboratory (JPL), responsible for mission operations, used the metric system (newton-seconds) for calculations and communication with spacecraft.

The **mismatch between imperial and metric units resulted in incorrect calculations** of the spacecraft's trajectory and velocity during orbital insertion maneuvers.

This is the only image returned by the orbiter. It is an image of Mars.

On September 23, 1999, during the planned orbital insertion maneuver, the Mars Climate Orbiter went missing.

The failure was attributed to the spacecraft entering Mars' atmosphere too steeply and at a higher velocity than planned, leading to its destruction.

PageRank Patent

Very few people know that PageRank algorithm which is the first algorithm to be used by Google Search Engine was a USPTO patented algorithm and the patent rights expired only in 2019. The twist is Google was not the owner of PageRank patent.

This restricted other companies to use the same algorithm in their search engine. Google had several other variants of PageRank which they patented and are still valid.

PageRank patent does not belong to Google

Yes, PageRank patent does not belong to Google.

The original PageRank patent was issued in 1999 and was titled "US6285999B1 - Method for node ranking in a linked database". Moreover, the trademark rights of the word "PageRank" are with Google.

The PageRank algorithm was developed by Larry Page when he was a PhD students and was developed under the supervision of Professor Héctor García Molina. The development started in 1996 and was published in 1998.

Professor Héctor García Molina

The legal name of Larry Page is Lawrence Page as in the patent application. Larry Page and Sergey Brin was working on a Web Linking Project at Stanford University as part of their PhD research.

Note: Sergey Brin was not part of the patent but Google was founded by both Larry Page and Sergey Brin with equal rights.

PageRank was influenced by 3 major research works which was also cited by Larry Page:

Work on Citation Analysis by Eugene Garfield (early 1950)

Hyper Search by Massimo Marchiori from University of Padua, Italy

HITS by Jon Kleinberg from Cornell University in Early 1998

The rights of PageRank Patent was assigned to Stanford University. This is because PageRank algorithm was developed by Larry Page who was a PhD student at the time

Lesson: If you are an employee, any idea you come up with will be the property of your employer.

Google brought the exclusive usage rights for PageRank from Stanford University for 1.8 million shares of Google. Stanford University sold all shares in 2005 for $336M.

The PageRank patent expired on 9th January 2019.

Next Patent on PageRank

A modified version of PageRank was patented and is still valid. It was titled "US9165040B1 - Producing a ranking for pages using distances in a web-linked graph".

It was developed by Nissan Hajaj, Google Engineer and application was filed in 2006. The rights of this patent on Updated PageRank is valid till 7 July 2027.

This is the short and interesting story behind the Patent of PageRank that is the basis of Google.

Most Profitable Software Patents

Patents on Software, Algorithm and Data Structures are very profitable if it finds widespread use. For example, PageRank algorithm which was in use by Google was patented by Stanford University. Due to this single patent, Stanford University earned $338M.

These are some of the Most Profitable Software Patents:

INVENTION	OWNER	REVENUE
PageRank Algorithm	Stanford University	$338M (one-time stock)
Karmarkar's Algorithm	AT&T	$8.9M per partnership (Total: $270M+)
Lempel Ziv Welch Algorithm	Unisys	Partnerships + $7500 per license (Total: $200M+)

Patent on PageRank algorithm in 1999

- Patent issued in: 1999
- Invention: PageRank Algorithm
- Patent owner: Stanford University
- Inventor: Larry Page, Founder of Google
- Profit: $338M in 2005

PageRank algorithm is a well-known algorithm as the algorithm that powered Google Search Engine. Very few know that PageRank is a patented algorithm. It was patented in 1999 and was assigned to Stanford University as Larry Page (Inventor) was pursuing PhD at that time.

Google brough exclusive Licensing rights from Stanford University for the use of the Algorithm at the cost of $1.8M in stocks. Stanford University sold the Google stocks for 338 Million dollars in 2005.

The patenting rights on PageRank is over as of 2019. Google has patents on other search algorithms which were later integrated into Google's search engine.

Patent on Karmarkar's algorithm in 1985

- Patent issued in: 1985
- Invention: Karmarkar's Algorithm
- Patent owner: AT&T
- Inventor: Narendra Karmarkar
- Profit: $8.9M per partnership

Karmarkar's algorithm was the first polynomial time algorithm for solving linear programming problems. It was formulated by Narendra Karmarkar when he was a researcher at IBM, presented it at Stanford University and later, joined AT&T.

At AT&T, the power of the algorithm in practical problem was realized. Karmarkar's algorithm was patented in 1985 by AT&T (Employer of Karmarkar). It was a major trigger to the revolt of software patents in 1980s.

The computer system designed to run this algorithm was priced at $8.9M and its first customer was Pentagon.

Karmarkar's Algorithm was a milestone in Linear Programming and for several decades, no alternative was found. This made a unique situation and put AT&T at a significant advantage. Over 30 companies came to partner with AT&T which made is earn nearly $270M.

The patent was over in 2006 and can be used by anyone currently.

Lempel Ziv Welch (LZW) lossless data compression (Patented in 1985)

- Patent issued in: 1985
- Invention: Lempel Ziv Welch (LZW) algorithm
- Patent owner: Unisys
- Inventor: Jacob Ziv, Abraham Lempel and Terry Welch
- Profit: $7500 per license (Over $50M in total)

Lempel Ziv Welch (LZW) lossless data compression is a compression algorithm that is used in GIF format. It was patented in 1985 by the company Unisys.

In 1977 and 1978, Jacob Ziv and Abraham Lempel developed several compression techniques which where later refined by Terry Welch in 1983 and the resultant algorithm was named Lempel Ziv Welch algorithm.

The patent was first assigned to Sperry Corporation in 1985. In 1986, the company was merged with Burroughs Corporation and the new company was named Unisys.

Unisys got licensing agreements from over 100+ companies.

The patent rights were not enforced for some companies but later, one-time royalties were collected. It reduced the popularity of GIF at that time provided an alternative (PNG) was ready. The one-time licensing fees was $7500.

In total, Unisys is reported to have earned over $200M for this one patent.

Origin of Git

With fall of **BitKeeper** ...

Every developer has used Git once in their development career. The story of its origin is interesting.

Before 2002, no VCS was used of the development of Linux (the dominant open-source OS).

In **2002**, Linus Torvalds, the creator of Linux, initiated the use of a proprietary VCS called **BitKeeper**. However, later when BitKeeper's free-of-charge access was revoked, Linus set out to create his own **VCS**.

In **2005**, Linus released **Git**. Git's design prioritized speed, scalability, and the ability to handle distributed workflows with ease. Its distributed nature allowed developers to work offline, branch and merge seamlessly, and collaborate across geographical boundaries effectively.

Git quickly gained popularity beyond the Linux community, becoming the de facto version control system for countless software projects, open-source initiatives, and enterprise environments.

BitKeeper was later released as an open-source project in **2016** and then, discontinued since **2018**.

Today, Git is the dominant player in VCS market.

Sad Story of Gerrit

GitHub's biggest unknown competitor ...

Gerrit is a web-based team code collaboration tool like GitHub. It is used by majority of BigTech companies but is gradually falling off.

Rietveld is a web-based collaboration tool developed by **Guido van Rossum** at Google in **2008**.

As the requirements grew with Android open-source project (AOSP) and Access Control List (ACL) could not be implemented with Rietveld, a new tool was needed.

Gerrit was created as a fork of Rietveld by **Shawn Pearce** at Google in **2009**.

Both Rietveld and Gerrit was named after Dutch designer **Gerrit Rietveld**. He designed multiple things like chairs and house.

```
$ git show 23571ab1fa7fedc262d6c21510614353e9d8a4dc

commit 23571ab1fa7fedc262d6c21510614353e9d8a4dc
Author: Shawn O. Pearce <s...@google.com>
Date:   Fri Nov 14 16:56:58 2008 -0800

    Initial project setup of Gerrit 2

    Gerrit 2 is a ground-up rewrite of Gerrit, using GWT (Google Web
    Toolkit) for the client side user interface and a Java servlet
    based backend.

    Signed-off-by: Shawn O. Pearce <s...@google.com>
```

This is the reason why Google did not acquire GitHub and Microsoft made its entry into open-source with GitHub's acquisition.

Sad news is:

Shawn Pearce, long-time Git contributor and founder of the Gerrit Code Review project, passed away at the young age of 39 over the last weekend in January 2018 after being diagnosed with lung cancer in 2017.

He was the founder of Gerrit and JGit at Google and was an exceptional contributor to open-source projects.

Google vs Oracle: 10 years long battle

It started in 2005 when Google included about 11,500 lines of code from Oracle's Java API in its Android operating system. Oracle, which purchased Sun Microsystems, the developer of the Java API, in 2010.

Following the acquisition, Oracle sued Google in 2010 for using Java's API without any license.

The case went through multiple rounds of litigation, including district court trials and appeals.

In 2012, a district court ruled that APIs were not subject to copyright protection. However, an appeals court overturned this decision in 2014, stating that APIs could be copyrighted.

Supreme Court and Fair Use:

Google petitioned the U.S. Supreme Court to review the case, and in 2015, the Supreme Court declined to hear it.

The case returned to the district court to determine if Google's use of Java APIs constituted fair use under copyright law.

In 2016, a jury found that Google's use of Java APIs in Android was considered fair use. Oracle was seeking $9B in damages and reappealed the case.

In 2018, United States Court of Appeals for the Federal Circuit ruled in favor of Oracle claiming the commercial use of APIs did not fall under fair use. Google filed a petition with the Supreme Court of the United States in January 2019 to challenge the ruling.

Finally in April 2021, the Supreme Court ruled in favor of Google in its 10-year legal battle with Oracle with a 6 to 2 majority decision.

Pentium Floating Point Division bug

The Pentium FDIV (Floating-Point Division) bug scandal occurred in **1994** and involved a critical error in Intel's Pentium microprocessors.

Bug Details:

- **Discovery**: The bug was discovered by **Thomas Nicely**, a professor of mathematics at **Lynchburg College**, who noticed discrepancies in calculations while running intensive computations on his Pentium-based computer in June 1994.
- **Bug Type**: The flaw was related to the FDIV instruction, which is used for floating-point division operations. It caused incorrect results in a small number of specific division calculations, resulting in rounding errors.

Documentation of FDIV assembly instruction:

FDIV/FDIVP/FIDIV — Divide

Opcode	Instruction	64-Bit Mode	Compat/Leg Mode	Description
D8 /6	FDIV m32fp	Valid	Valid	Divide ST(0) by m32fp and store result in ST(0).
DC /6	FDIV m64fp	Valid	Valid	Divide ST(0) by m64fp and store result in ST(0).
D8 F0+i	FDIV ST(0), ST(i)	Valid	Valid	Divide ST(0) by ST(i) and store result in ST(0).
DC F8+i	FDIV ST(i), ST(0)	Valid	Valid	Divide ST(i) by ST(0) and store result in ST(i).
DE F8+i	FDIVP ST(i), ST(0)	Valid	Valid	Divide ST(i) by ST(0), store result in ST(i), and pop the register stack.
DE F9	FDIVP	Valid	Valid	Divide ST(1) by ST(0), store result in ST(1), and pop the register stack.
DA /6	FIDIV m32int	Valid	Valid	Divide ST(0) by m32int and store result in ST(0).
DE /6	FIDIV m16int	Valid	Valid	Divide ST(0) by m16int and store result in ST(0).

- **Magnitude**: The error was rare, affecting less than one in a billion floating-point calculations. However, given the millions of Pentium processors in circulation, it raised concerns about the chip's reliability for scientific, engineering, and financial calculations.
- **Public Outcry**: Nicely's findings were publicized in an Internet newsgroup, sparking widespread criticism and media attention. Users and industry experts demanded a response from Intel regarding the severity of the issue and its potential impact.

Intel's Response:

Initial Response: Intel initially downplayed the significance of the bug, stating that it was "a minor problem" that would rarely affect typical users and they were aware of it.

- **Escalation**: As public outcry grew and pressure mounted, Intel faced escalating criticism from customers, industry analysts, and the media.
- **Resolution Efforts**: In November 1994, Intel announced a program to address the issue, offering free replacements or refunds to affected customers who could demonstrate a need for accurate floating-point calculations.

- **Financial Impact**: The Pentium FDIV bug scandal resulted in significant financial losses for Intel, with estimates ranging from **$475 million to $500 million for the replacement program** and associated costs.
- **Long-Term Impact**: The incident prompted Intel to implement more rigorous testing and quality control measures in its processor development process. It also underscored the importance of transparency and responsiveness in handling hardware issues affecting customers.

Overall, the Pentium FDIV bug scandal highlighted the complexities and challenges of semiconductor manufacturing, emphasizing the need for thorough validation and testing to ensure the reliability and accuracy of microprocessors.

Apple's breakup with Intel after 15 years

2005 to 2021

Casual link between Apple and Intel dates back to 1980s but both got into a firm partnership in 2005.

Early Collaborations and Shifts:

- Early Partnership: Intel and Apple's collaboration dates back to the 1980s when Apple used Intel processors in certain Macintosh computers, transitioning from Motorola processors.
- PowerPC Era: In the mid-1990s, Apple shifted to using PowerPC processors developed by IBM, Motorola resulting in Apple's joint venture, AIM (Apple, IBM, Motorola).
- Start of **Intel x Apple**: In **2005**, Apple announced a **significant transition from PowerPC to Intel processors**, citing performance, power efficiency, and software compatibility reasons.

Collaboration Highlights:

- Macintosh with Intel Processors: Apple's transition to Intel processors began with the Macintosh lineup, including the MacBook Pro, iMac, and Mac mini, offering improved performance and compatibility.
- Thunderbolt Technology: Intel collaborated with Apple to develop Thunderbolt, a high-speed I/O technology used in Mac computers, enabling fast data transfer and connectivity with external devices.

- Chipset Development: Apple worked closely with Intel on chipset development for Mac computers, optimizing performance, power management, and integration with macOS.

Rivalry and Legal Disputes:

- iPhone Modem Supply: Intel entered the smartphone modem market and secured a contract to supply modems for certain iPhone models, challenging Qualcomm's dominance.
- Legal Battles: Apple and Qualcomm engaged in legal disputes over patent licensing and royalty fees, leading Apple to seek alternative modem suppliers like Intel.
- Intel's Struggles: Intel faced challenges in meeting Apple's performance and quality standards for modems, leading to issues with speed, reliability, and power consumption in iPhones using Intel modems.

Shifts in Partnership and Intel's Exit:

- Settlement with Qualcomm: In 2019, Apple and Qualcomm settled their legal disputes and reached an agreement for Qualcomm to supply modems for future iPhones.
- Intel exited the smartphone modem business and **Apple acquired Intel's modem business** and associated 2200 Intel employees for **$1B in July 2019.**
- Apple still used Intel processors in Macs at this point, this resulted in up to **$3B per year in revenue for Intel** which was around 4% of Intel's total revenue.

Final days

- In November 2020, Apple announced its own ARM based System on Chip (SoC) named Apple M1.
- On 26 October 2021, Apple announced M1 Pro and M1 Max and discontinued all Macs with Intel chips **bringing the 15 years old partnership with Intel to an END.**
- The **Mac Operating System** still supports Intel processors (for backward compatibility so old users can update the OS). Apple has not confirmed when the support will end but may suggest Mac OS 16 set to be released in 2025 may not support Intel processors at all.
- On 5 June 2023, Apple announced their transition from Intel is complete and on **5 June 2028**, Intel hardware will be given "**vintage**" status and on **5 June 2030**, it will be given "**obsolete**" status.

KEEP ENJOYING COMPUTER SCIENCE

www.ingramcontent.com/pod-product-compliance
Lightning Source LLC
Chambersburg PA
CBHW031554210526
45464CB00003B/1293